SORROW, JOY & SELF-REFLECTION

POEMS

KYLE BRADLEY

Copyright © 2018 Kyle Bradley
All rights reserved

Cover Photos by:
Dikaseva on Unsplash
Tuân Nguyễn Minh on Unsplash

THANK YOU

To everyone who loved, listened, encouraged and held us.

CONTENTS

1. A New Year
3. You Lying There
4. Apart
6. My Two Selves
8. Pleading
11. Talking to Myself
13. Alive and Bright
14. Venting
15. Not Even a Bit
16. Could it Be
18. Much More
22. The Moments Between
26. Closer
28. Watching
29. Hope and Expectation
30. Why it Hurts
31. Anxiety
33. Why Do Things
34. Cracks in the Dam
37. Bleeding
38. Refusal
39. Without You

40. Fading

41. A Wish

42. Morning at the Lake

44. October 15

47. October 16

49. In a Moment

52. Castle

53. Land of Grief

54. Circular

55. Spreading

56. Hatred

60. They'll Come Back

62. Drawing Me Out

63. I'm Not Sure I Know

66. Friday, January 20

67. How Do I Describe it?

70. Can't

71. November 15

73. November 16

74. More Than

75. Better

76. The Healer

77. Back

78. Filling in Blanks

79. November 28 - What Ifs

81. Can't Wait Another Day

82. Beaten Over Time

84. A Great Strength in Him

86. Between Moments of Grief

88. Hear and See

90. I Wonder

91. A River

93. Stop

94. People Pleaser

95. Another Version

96. Internal Dislike

97. None

99. Walls

100. Comfortably

101. Growing Love

102. Something I Hate

103. Reflection

104. 32 Years

105. Two Words

106. …Then Today Happened

109. Why, Brother

110. Unsure

111. Processing

112. Unknowing

113. A Voice in the Dark

114. Held

116. Experiment

117. Need of You

118. Not Okay

119. Thinking Back

120. A Question

121. Thankful

122. Fear

123. Too Many

124. Paranoia

125. Falling Over the Edge

126. Lost and Alone

127. My Heart

128. Almost

129. What Death Says

130. Between You and Me

131. Will and Why

132. End and Beginning

A NEW YEAR

Five

Four

Three

Two

One

'16 is over

A new year has begun

Full of familiar

   but ripe with possibility

Learning

   and growing

   and loving

But death changes everything

21 days in

A loss

A great loss

A mom

A cornerstone for family

And six months in

   two more

A grandma

An aunt

A year that looked bright

Shattered

  destroyed

Full of heartache

A year of loss

  but not a year lost

For good would come in month 10

Filling a space

  where only sorrow had been

Overflowing joy

  in the shape of baby

A second, sweet little boy

Born October 16

Changing my year

And after three losses

Three deaths

Reshaping my life

And my heart

Making them bright…

…then today happened

YOU LYING THERE

I can't escape it

outrun or unthink it

a thought

a picture

that destroys me

strangles

paralyzes

shatters

beautiful and broken

you lying there

fading

and a piece of my heart

with you

dying

APART

Frozen

Watching

A world that won't stop moving

A blur of focused energy

A determined hurricane

I stand in its eye

   alone and lost

     a part of it

        apart

Early on it slowed

Slowed enough

   that someone might break free

   from the everything

To stand in the eye

To step into my heart

   and feel the broken pieces

To soak in my tears

   and feel the depths

     of sorrow and loss

To know the fullness of love

Ripped away in a moment

And then back
   to the hurricane
   to responsibilities
But maybe another would come
   to sit and listen
     or hold me for a time
     before returning

And it's not long
Before the winds pick up
   and they stop coming
Caught in the everything
   apart
Except for the few
The determined
Who force their way through
   the wind
     and my facade
       and my defenses
And lovingly help
   pick up the pieces

MY TWO SELVES

It's difficult
facing the realities of me
my weaknesses
and shortcomings
I subconsciously hide from everyone
especially myself
until they become so strong
so apparent
the energy it takes
to bury them
disguise them
avoid or destroy them
is too much
and I'm left facing the one
I'd rather not be
the anxious, scared and angry self
longing for the other
the calm, confident, fearless self
I would always choose the one
but I can't choose what isn't real
so instead
I face reality

for the first time
trying to be comfortable
with who I am
enough to let others
see the real me

PLEADING

Frozen in time

Unmoving

Unbelieving

Watching

You

Breathing

But gone

Though you didn't seem gone

And that's what was hard

You just looked asleep

Because your eyes were closed

And you looked at peace

A machine

Pumping air

Your chest rising slowly

Then falling

Asleep

But not

Just kept alive

But not

Only enough so they could take parts of you

To give to others

Who might have more time
Really, you were already gone
But I couldn't accept it
I wouldn't accept it
I was a statue
With a storm raging inside
Trying to look strong
For others
For me
Why?
I thought
Why?
WHY?!!
Why?
JUST OPEN YOUR EYES!!

Frozen in time
Pleading inside
Pleading
And pleading
and pleading
Why?!!
WHY?!!!!
Move something!
A finger!

A toe!

Give us a sign!

Open your eyes!!

and smile

you're fine

You can't die!

YOU CAN'T DIE!!!

this

can't

be

goodbye

TALKING TO MYSELF

I'm afraid

Of what?

A lot

Why?

I don't know exactly
   but I'm tired of it
I'm tired because of it
I can't seem to change it
Can't think myself out of it

Try to name it

Perfection
Failure
The need to be perfect
The fear of falling
   even a fraction short

Who says you need to be perfect?

Me

Anyone else?

No
Only me
And it's exhausting
Each moment
Chasing something that can't be caught
Afraid of something only I can see

How would it feel to not care?
How would it feel to be free?

ALIVE AND BRIGHT

I don't often remember
The things in the night
The time
The moments
In dreams while I sleep

But sometimes I remember
When I dream of you
Sitting or walking
Or talking with me
No longer gone
But alive and bright
And for that moment
Everything feels whole, like before
Everything feels right

But it doesn't last
Because I wake
And lie there
Clinging to the dream
Like holding water
Missing you

VENTING

How dare you

Question me

Or question my grief

You're not me

And don't know how it should be

When things should feel normal

And I should return

Completely

Do you even care enough

To not ask someone else

But ask me about me

To see me as more than a tool

To accomplish the things that you need

Do you know how much I hurt

How many restless nights

How much I cry

How my life has felt

Like it's falling apart

And how hard it can be

To accomplish anything

NOT EVEN A BIT

Blah

Blah

Blah

Blah

Blah

I don't care

COULD IT BE

Could it be

That I've checked out

And checked in

To apathy

Tired of grief

Of being stressed

And filled with anxiety

That I've abandoned any feeling

And only exist

Free of the things

That bruise my heart

And the fear that drains

I've checked out

And checked in

Could it be

That in doing so

I've forgotten how to live

To really care

And laugh

And love

To see joy and good

In countless small
Beautiful things
Things that matter
The eternal

MUCH MORE

I'm quick to do

All the things that come naturally

That come easy

Why not be quick?

Those things make me look good

Those things make me feel good

I'm good at those things

But what about the rest

Of the "things"

I don't even like to think about them

When I do

They scare me

Because if I try

I know the outcome

A failure?

Maybe

But likely not entirely

Or not at all

Likely just something I'll struggle with

That won't come easy

That I'm not good at

And won't end as well as I'd like

That will be far from perfect

Not a failure, I think

By others' standards

But some sort of failure

By my own

By my unrealistic standards

By the expectations

I've unconsciously set

The result of doing only the easy

So…

Maybe

I'm in a kind of stuckness

A constant state of ungrowth

It doesn't look bad after all

Outwardly

Because the things I choose to do

They look good

Arrogant?

Maybe

Really just terrified

To step out of the comfortable

To fail on any level

And face the worst of judges

Me

Because let's be real

Others

Are much more forgiving

And gracious

Toward me than me

So I'm left

Shaking and anxious

Like a scared little kid

Trying not to face the bad guy

The bully

My own mocking voice saying,

  "You're stupid

  inadequate

  unqualified

  ugly

  a coward

  a bad friend

  worse husband and father

  you're nothing"

  and more

It has for most of my life

So, I cling to what I do

The easy

Terrified to jump

Into the difficult

The uncomfortable

The hardest place to go
But the place where I know
Real growth comes from
Honesty comes from
Vulnerability
That I'm not what you see
Or what I want to be
I'm the scared little kid
Good at some things
Mediocre at others
Bad at a lot
But I'm not
What the awful voice says
I am much more than that
The good and the bad
The successes and failures
The imperfections
The not-even-trying
I'm much more than the lies
It would have me believe
I'm enough

I am me

THE MOMENTS BETWEEN

The big things are great

Those not easily forgotten

The ones worth countless pictures

Trips to the happiest place on earth

    Smells of popcorn and sweets

    Sounds of laughter and booming fireworks

    Rides and shows

Or vacations at the beach

    Salt in the air

    Feet sinking slowly in wet sand

    Rhythmic waves rolling

Or holidays

    With costumes and candy

    And cookies and gifts

    Pumpkins and turkey

    Midnight with friends

These things are great

When lasting memories are made

But it's the moments between

The things more easily forgotten

I tightly hold on to

That make life so special

The ordinary

The routine

Spectacular

So very sweet

It's holding hands on the couch

   With my beautiful

   My best friend

   My bride

It's piggy back rides with my son

   And wrestling matches

   And flying him around like Superman

It's silly voices

   And pirate songs

   And dancing in the living room

It's racing cars

   And building blocks

   And wooden tracks with trains

It's late-night wakings

   His little voice calling

   And snuggling with him

      until he falls asleep again

It's family hugs

   And I love yous

   And kisses before bed

It's building forts

  And hide and seek
It's the anticipation of going home
  Rounding the corner
   and seeing them
  Their smiling faces
  Happy we're together again
It's jammies and sweats
  Movies and popcorn
  Saturday pancakes
  And walks at sunset
It's laughing
  And running
  And messy-hair mornings
It's reading books
  And playing games
  And watching his favorite cartoons
It's working around the house
  Or out in the yard
  With him by my side
  Little tools in little hands
   just wanting to help his dad
It's her smile
  And the way she lights up
   when they play together
  Or when he says

  I love you mommy
It's waking up
 And going to sleep
 Knowing she's next to me
It's dreaming together
 And holding each other
  When grief and sorrow come calling
 And with them, tears
  and more fear
 Safe and comfortable arms
It's car rides
 And coffee runs
It's date nights
 Or mornings
 Just the two of us
 Talking and laughing
It's each moment
 I get to be
  with her
  with him
  together

CLOSER

the dark before the dawn

empty streets

blinking lights

cold air teasing fall

a new day

much like the day before

longing of a conflicted heart

pulled between grief and joy

hiding from reality

for fear of the first

and missing the second

light creeps over the horizon

brighter and brighter

warmer

and joy tries to join it

sneaking

spreading carefully

over a heart like the dark

like the cold

looking for weaknesses

along an invisible wall

knowing what's best
to break through
and rise like the sun
filling everything with light
but there's no opening
so joy paces slowly
searching
biding its time
closer to the surface
than the day before

WATCHING

I'm on the outside

watching my life

pass

me

by

HOPE AND EXPECTATION

I've hoped for more from you
I've expected more from you
And all you do is disappoint
But I probably just disappoint, too

WHY IT HURTS

It hurts

So much

Because of love

Real

Honest

Selfless love

It hurts

So much

Because a little wasn't lost

A great deal was

A lifetime

Cut short

ANXIETY

My enemy

Ever-present

Holding me back

Taking control

Hiding

Disguised as my protector

Cunning and calculated

Sometimes coming on quick

When I least expect it

Other times

Creeping

Teasing for days

Weeks

Months

For something coming

Something it knows I fear

Or something I don't

That it convinces me to

Lurking in the shadows

Plotting and pulling

Pricking and cutting

Twisting the truth

Building

And before I realize it

It breaks free from the darkness

Wrapping itself around me

Overwhelming me

Crippling

Heart pounding

Sweat pouring

Unmoving

It wins

WHY DO THINGS

Consumed with the doing
To avoid the not moving
  and the thinking
  and over-thinking
To avoid the heartache
  and the grief
  and the tears
  and the loss

CRACKS IN THE DAM

Sad truths

Harsh realities

A broken world

Death

Abuse

Disease

Too much

So

I avoid these things

Or try to

Hiding behind what?

Selfishness

Dreams

Fantasies

Not wanting to feel sadness

Damming up

Pushing down

Not feeling

Until

Without my knowing

Something shifts

A fraction

A crack in the stone

A hairline slice

And a trickle of sadness

Almost nothing

  but enough

And ever so slowly

  the crack spreads, multiplies

Like veins in marble

No longer nothing

I sense it

The leaks in my dam

The threat of destruction

The fear

That the veins will become holes

And the stone will crumble

So, I push harder

I press my hands against it

  to stop each leak

But 10 fingers aren't enough

And I can't avoid forever

I can't hold it back

Then something unexpected

Something small and sad triggers it

And my trying isn't enough

And in an instant

Cracks and holes gape

Sadness rushes out

Water fills my eyes

And my blinking is a last-ditch effort

But the wall comes down

And sorrow like a flood

   washes over me

And there's nothing left to do

But to shake

And to weep

BLEEDING

Maybe I should give you the benefit of the doubt
That the hurtful things you say and think
That in some way
They aren't really directed at me
Or at least
Not with the intention to truly hurt
That before you threw them out
You just didn't think
How all your words would be perceived

And you speak without knowing the real me
So maybe you don't know
That what you say
More than just stings
The words you carelessly toss
They cut
And I bleed

REFUSAL

today

i won't be sorry

i'm not interested

my aunt
my grandma
my mom

they're dead

they're gone

so, I don't care

not today

WITHOUT YOU

Where would I be
Without you
  with me
Lost and alone
And hopeless
I think

FADING

I see her in others

In gestures

In smiles

I see her in my rearview mirror

I see her when I close my eyes

But I see her less as time goes by

And I cry

I'm afraid

That her face

Her smile

Memories of her

Will escape me

And I'll try and I'll try

But won't ever fully recall

A WISH

I miss you
   and wish
We could talk and get lunch
Just like before
Or that I could hug you
And hear you say
   I love you buddy

MORNING AT THE LAKE

Water like glass

A ripple here

A ripple there

From fish gone back under

Hardly disturbed

Fog resting gently atop

Hiding the far shore

Rocks and trees

The sun inching over dark green

Birds chirp and sing

Or glide feet above the glass

A motor kicks on

A low rumble

Distant

Then close

A fisherman

His boat slicing like a knife

Flying

And in a moment, gone

Out of site

A distant rumble again

It's wake spreading wide

Fading against the rocky shore

Everything settling

And glass reflecting beauty once more

OCTOBER 15

A mixture
  of nerves and anticipation
After weeks
  and months of waiting
    moving furniture
    building a crib
    arranging clothes
    and painting
It's after 10
  room 5617
  we're settled in
And I look at her
  my love
  my bride
  my best friend
Lying there
  as beautiful as ever
  tucked in
    for what could be a long night ahead
And I can't help but feel
  admiration and pride
    and so much more

Thankfulness and joy
   that I get to live life
      with this amazing woman
      and get to watch her with our boy
I look at her
   and my heart overflows
I look at her
   and see so much
So much strength
   compassion
   courage
   love
I see an incredible wife
   and friend and mother
Thinking of herself last
   long after she thinks of others
I see the one
   that makes each moment special
      memorable and sweet
Beyond what I'd imagined
   far past what I could dream
I watch her lying there
   hours still to go
Waiting to welcome our second
   another precious little boy

And I can't imagine it any different
I wouldn't change a thing
  because my life with her
    it's perfect
Every moment
Every up and down
Every laugh and tear
Everything
  is sweet

OCTOBER 16

New life

Tears in eyes

His and mine

Little hands and ears

   and button nose

Little feet

   with the cutest little toes

Joy

Her smile

Beautiful

Bright

Watching him in my arms

   after a long, hard night

He's my life

My love

My third perfect

One, my wife

   My love

   My life

Two, our firstborn son

   Full of personality

   So sweet

    So fun
And three, our new little boy
    So precious and small
    Already filling us with joy

IN A MOMENT

Grief is a sneaky thing

For months it seems you've dealt with it

It's gone perhaps

You've moved past

or bested it

How foolish you can be

to think it's gone

in just a few short months

As easy as can be

But grief is a fickle thing

and not something to defeat

You busy yourself

doing this or that

You fear showing your broken heart

to the people around you

So, you suppress it

avoiding a downpour of tears

Not sure they can face it

the depths of your sorrow

Certain you can't

You send it away

like an unwelcome guest

And you trick yourself

for a time

thinking everything's all right

everything is fine

And then something happens

A trigger

A spotlight

And everything comes rushing back

Your life begins to skid

You feel out of control

and the tears begin to fall

For me

that moment was a baby

My second son

So sweet and precious

One day old

and full of hope

He sleeps

and I watch him

And after a day of pure joy

with family and friends

celebrating him

my eyes fill with tears

and I shake

Because when I look at him
I think of her
My mom
His granny
And how she isn't here
To love him
To hug and kiss him
and watch him through the years
And my heart
that overflows with joy
for my sweet little boy
overflows with sorrow
for the loss of my mother
And that in this life
he will never know her

CASTLE

My home

A building, sure

Brick, wood and glass

But so much more

Especially with them

It transforms

A sanctuary

Beautiful and warm and safe

Not just from the elements

The wind and cold and rain

But from my enemies

The invisible, lurking just beyond our door

    Fear

    Doubt

    Anxiety

    Embarrassment

    Insecurity and

    Shame

  Holding so much over me

  Such great power in their names

But I can't stay inside forever

Where love and walls keep them out

LAND OF GRIEF

How do I grieve?
With so much to do
So much depending on me
When I don't want to think
Don't want to be
When there's no easy way
No a, b, or c
No way that feels right
When everything's wrong
Up feels down
Light feels dark
Full becomes stark
A map with no lines
No end in sight
No way to feel free
Lost here
Lost in my grief

CIRCULAR

How do I wake

Open my eyes

And rise

From this place

This wasted state

Where grief came from death

And turned to apathy

Then anger

And back

And again

And again

And again

SPREADING

The poison of anxiety
Is eating at me
And spreading
Like weeds

Like a disease

HATRED

Feeling empty

A darkness so heavy

Remembering another time

A long time

Years ago

When darkness reigned

Crept through my veins

And consumed

For years I tried to hide it

From others

And myself

Tried hard to present a version
   of myself that didn't struggle

Thinking people would wonder
   what's wrong with me

But the darkness
   heavy and terrible and
   filled with a voice

An unforgiving

Unrelenting voice

My voice
   but not me

This darkness filled my everything
This voice attacked every inch
Destroying me

I remember, with sorrow
Standing
Hands gripping the edge of the sink
Knuckles white
Head hanging
Tears filling
And thinking

And thinking

Then slowly
   raising my head

Looking

And really looking

At the person I hated most in the world
Hated more than anything
Tears rolled down my cheeks
And the voice raged inside of me

Saying the most hateful things
Things I'd never say to another
Things too terrible to repeat

Heart pounding
Lungs heaving
I erupted
And hate and rage poured out
I lifted my hand
Making a fist
And looked at myself again
With loathing, with sorrow
And I swung
As hard as I could
My fist slamming into my eye
Like hitting raw meat
And again with a thud
And again and again and again
Ears ringing
My fist on repeat
And after who knows how many times
I looked at my bruised and broken face
Then sank to the ground
   and cried

And for years I lied about that day

Lied about me

Told a story

Acted in a way that people believed

To afraid to reveal the real me

The one who wanted to hide

From everything

And for years

The one who wanted to die

THEY'LL COME BACK

Grief sucks

Because death is worse

But grief isn't the only

And death isn't final

It's there

At times you can't feel it

Can't see it

But hope is there

Joy can be found

The sun will rise

Bringing flowers from dead ground

Newness

Life

Laughter

Love

Things thought lost or gone

They'll come back

If you let them

They'll embrace you

And you'll move on

Different

But on

With

And without

Because death is worse

Loved ones will die

But they will live on

Here

And there

Your heart and mind

And more

DRAWING ME OUT

I'm drawn to the things

creative things

that make me feel

That overwhelm

and make me think

Good or bad

High highs

Low lows

Why?

I think…

deep in me

there's a longing to feel deeply

To step out of the shallows

and be overwhelmed

That feels like living

fully alive

And maybe not feeling

the lowest lows

and highest highs

For me,

maybe…

that's not even being

I'M NOT SURE I KNOW

Most of the time

My waking life

Something holds

Something binds

Threatening my demise

If only I were unaware of it

Enjoying bliss from ignorance

I could handle that

Not knowing it exists

This constant worry and fear of it

Of embarrassment

Nearly every choice

Every step

Every word

Is made with this in mind

And because of this

This fear of embarrassment

There's so much I avoid

So much I miss

And I think

To what extent

Does it keep me from being me

Or is this fearful

Unmoving one

Thinking

And over-thinking

Is this the best version of me I'm meant to be

Irrationally, maybe

Logically, no

But I guess I care so much

About what other people think

How I'm perceived

That I sometimes avoid

Even the smallest of things

Because I'm afraid I'll be judged

I fear what they'll think

So, the me that I am

Most of the time

Is the one I think they want me to be

And the truth is

I think I'm putting too much on them

Because my guess is they don't care

About my pretending and trying

They'd accept the real me

But that's easy to say and easy to think

And if so

If I accepted that

Felt the freedom of that
How would it change me
Inside and out?
Who would I be?

FRIDAY, JANUARY 20

If I had known a Friday

Would be the last time

That I'd get to say goodbye

That on Saturday she'd lose her life

Would I have changed anything about that night?

No, I think

With tears in eyes

Because that last visit was a special one

A visit full of things she loved

With people she loved

It's hard to think about my final words

Our last moments

Our final hug

And "I love you"

An entire evening

A last memory

Of her alive

A memory

Still so fresh

It makes me smile

And makes me cry

HOW DO I DESCRIBE IT?

Nine pounds

And three weeks old

So beautiful

Perfect

My Mushmellow

Your resting against my legs

Your head in my hands

Your eyes looking

Exploring

And I watch you

Enthralled

In love

Overcome

And thankful

That I get to be your dad

I pull you close

Gently

So close

I breathe you in

And I watch you

Your beautiful gray-blue eyes

Moving left to right

Right to left

And back again

But once

For a moment

They stop

And rest on mine

You see me

And I see you

Everything disappears

There's nothing else outside

Just me

And you

So much emotion, love and pride

Stop

Fast forward a bit

I sit here and think

Pencil in hand

And I'm at a loss

I don't know what to write

Because the amount of love I feel for you

It seems I can't describe

And I know

Whatever I put on paper
Will pale
Then disappear in comparison
To what I felt inside

When I think about the moment
Your eyes locked onto mine

CAN'T

Would you come find me

I'm lost inside myself

Lost

And hurting

And I know

All I have to do

Is just reach out to you

Ask you

Would you help me

Would you listen

And hold me

But sometimes it seems I can't

NOVEMBER 15

I sit
In a crowded room
People I care about
Who care about me
But I don't care
To try and pretend
Or try to be
Who I think you think I should be

Normally
I'd be uncomfortable
Afraid to sit quietly
A shell of a me
So I'd force myself
To jump in
Make jokes
And contribute
To avoid this feeling
Of being empty

But today is different
I sit in a group

Feeling completely alone
Alien, almost
And I don't want to try
I just want to be
To feel real
So, I do nothing
And I sit in the feeling
Quietly
Content to not speak
And for a bit
If only for a bit
I feel free

NOVEMBER 16

It's late
It's dark
Heavy eyes
Heavy heart
But sleep won't come
So I lie here and think
Your birthday tomorrow
Wishing we could celebrate
Laugh and eat cake
Wishing for one more day
   that can't be

MORE THAN

I love you, son
More than you'll ever know
Or at least until
You have a little boy or girl of your own

BETTER

I hope for you both
That you're only a part of me
That you don't have my insecurities
My doubts
And anxieties
I hope these things
Will pass you by
That you'll be braver than me
Confident
Defenders
Of yourselves
and others
That you'll be the best of me
And better than the rest of me

THE HEALER

Time heals all wounds

Easy to say

Easy to think

But it doesn't bring the dead back to life

It doesn't wipe the tears from my eyes

I almost hate it

Because I feel

That all time does

Is make me forget

Like some cheap kind of trick

And I cling

To memories

And the more I forget

The more time between

The easier it will be

And it's frustrating to think

That even now

As it passes by

My wounds might be healing

BACK

I wish I could go back in time
To January 21
I wish I were there
To catch you
To cradle your head in my hands
And save you from the fall
That took you from us
Took you from all

FILLING IN BLANKS

What does honesty look like?

Not just telling the truth about this or that

But honesty that comes from

The desire to be known

REALLY and **TRULY** known

With no mask

No pretending

Or conforming

With no fear of…

Or worry that…

NOVEMBER 28 - WHAT IFS

What if things were different
If we had done something
Changed something
Taken a different path
That might've led to a different result
What if you had stopped working
What if you hadn't felt dizzy
Or climbed on the ladder
What if you had fallen differently
Landed differently
What if you weren't on blood thinners
Hadn't had brain surgery a year before
What if they had gotten there faster
Or tried something different
What if it were a different hospital
With different doctors
What if there was a way
A way that wouldn't lead to your death
There's an endless supply of what ifs
That might have changed it
But what ifs don't help
They're a fantasy that just make this harder

And in the end
What if it was just your time

CAN'T WAIT ANOTHER DAY

Awkward

Nervous

So outside my comfort zone

But something I must say

Something I must own

Because I care too much about you

About us

To go on

Without saying what I need to say

Hoping you'll be willing to hear

Because it's important

And can't wait another day

BEATEN OVER TIME

A flower

Growing

Beautiful

Withstanding the elements

But not unchanged

Beaten by a strong wind

Relentless

Uncaring as it pushes

And slowly

Over time

A pedal falls

And then another

Still beautiful

And vibrant

But the wind

It never stops

Not completely

And any respite

Any calm

Only gives false hope

That maybe it's gone

But the wind

It's never gone
And one by one
More pedals fall
Until there are none
Until beauty is gone

A GREAT STRENGTH IN HIM

Strength in his tears

Thinking of so many years

Strength in his silence

Behind his eyes

Strength in his weakness

In his mourning

In his loss

And he lost the most

He lost his love

His best friend

His bride

Great plates shifted

And rocked his world

And everything changed

Changed the most for him

Because at the end of the day

When my tears have dried

I still get to be home with my boys

With my wife

But he walks alone

Through empty halls

Empty rooms

An empty home

He lies down

And there's nothing beside him

But cold sheets

He lies down to no one

And nothing to keep him company

Except for his thoughts

But despite all that

He tries to stay strong

He prays and hopes

And each day he goes on

BETWEEN MOMENTS OF GRIEF

More time between
The tears in my eyes
The hiding and crying
So people don't see
My broken heart
On the outside of me

More time between
The tears in my eyes
But when they come
They come worse than before
When they came so very often
When the wound was fresh

And maybe some time
Sooner or later
There will be
Even more time between
And it will be easier than now
Than before
Fewer tears
From a heart that's mending

Never to be whole again

But healthier

With scar tissue

Signs of my grief

Of your life's impact on me

HEAR AND SEE

If only there were some way

Some way to have known

The things I now know

If only some way

To have been warned

A year ago

Or three or four

Or more

Could something good have been better

I don't know

Because we were always so close

But if I had known then

What I know now

I'd like to think

That I'd have done more

Asked her more

Taken less for granted

Like the amount of time we aren't guaranteed

Because now

Right now

In this moment

I wish more than anything

That I could just sit next to her
And listen to her laugh
Or complain
Or tell stories
I just wish
More than anything
I could hear her
Hear the love in her voice
And see her
The light in her eyes
The lines on her cheeks
When she smiled
And she smiled wide
She was beautiful
And so was her life
Her impact on others
And I just want more time
But the reality is heavy
So unbelievably heavy
And I just try not to forget
I sit by myself
I write
And I cry

I WONDER

Is it gone?

I wonder

The stuff of kids

Stolen

By life

By time

And the world

The hopes

And dreams

And fantasies

Things we were destined to think

And invent

Creativity

A RIVER

Below the surface

Sometimes far

Sometimes just

A current flows

That never completely runs out

Or dries up

A part

That most don't see

The nine in me

A current of anger

Anger I don't often understand

That maybe comes

From my own failures and disappointments

From a life thrown into chaos

From a lack of control

Over the things around me

Anger from an unhealthy view of myself

That I can't be

Who I'd really like to be

And often

I want more than anything

For this river of anger

To stop or just leave

But it ebbs and flows

And every so often

Pushes against

Begins to flood

Then explodes

But no one knows

Because the person

Who gets swept up with it

The one on the receiving end

Is me

Inwardly

And I fight

And silently scream

Attacking and abusing myself

Until it retreats

But it never completely subsides

Never dries, not really

And it cycles

Creeping over a river bed

A trickle

For a time

Until the things I don't fully understand

Bring on more rushing water

And it happens again

STOP

Could everyone stop

And be safe

So we don't lose anymore

PEOPLE PLEASER

Why can't I just not care
Why do I feel the need
To please everyone
To keep things peaceful
And fair

ANOTHER VERSION

I'm tired

Tired of performing

From the moment I wake

Till the moment I sleep

Much of the day

I exhaust myself

Just trying to be

Something or someone other than me

Plotting and planning

Moving and scheming

So whatever I do

I will look to you

Like someone who has it all together

Someone who looks better

Than how I feel

If you stop

And I stop

And we speak

You're probably not getting

The realest version of me

You're getting the manufactured one

The one it takes so much energy to be

INTERNAL DISLIKE

I could just stop
And be
Whatever
And not talk
Or think
And have peace
Existing in the silence
Because I'm tired of so much
Of my performing

You ask how I'm doing
And I give you
About as much as I think you can handle
Because there are times
I feel so much sorrow
So much dislike
So much that I'm afraid
You might see the hate through my eyes
In my mind
As I try to decide
Which piece of me is the worst

NONE

I have such little control

And sometimes it sucks

Because if I'm honest

All I really want to do

Deep down

Is control

Control every little thing

To try and maintain

Fabricated peace

And balance

And harmony

To feel happy

Because if I'm in control

Nothing can go wrong

Right?

So much energy

Physical

Mental

Trying to orchestrate my life

And the things around me

So I won't be scared

Or anxious

Or angry

So I won't have to worry

And face the reality

That so much controls me

And the power I have over things

Is nothing

WALLS

Perfection

Anxiety

Insecurity

Shame

Make up the four walls

Of a prison

Where I spend

Most of my days

COMFORTABLY

Only on rare occasions

In certain places

With certain faces

Do I ever feel

Completely comfortable in my own skin

And I wish

I could give myself permission

To stop caring

And just be me

Without worry

Or anxiety

To not let fear of anyone

And how they may judge me

Control what I do

Or control what I think

GROWING LOVE

It's late
After a night out
After our date
And we're home
And tired
But comfortable
Because home
Is our sanctuary
And our boys are there
Tucked in for the night
And we can't go to bed
Without sneaking
Into their rooms
And softly kissing
Each on his head
And whispering
I love you
And my heart soars
Because each day
I love them more

SOMETHING I HATE

Constantly thinking

And doing things

To never rock the boat

To never inconvenience

Or upset

Anyone

Or anything

REFLECTION

To look in a mirror
And love what I see
Would feel for the first time
Like I am free

32 YEARS

32 years

Of your laugh

Your voice

Your hugs

32 years of love

And now

Nothing

But what feels like

Fading memories

And all but forgotten

Moments

In between

TWO WORDS

Two words I said a thousand times
But never really said
For the most important things you did
Things I probably took for granted
And I wish you were still around to hear them
But you're not
So I'll write them down instead

Thank you

For your love
And the countless ways you showed it
Thank you for quality time
And making special
So much of my life
Thank you for the hugs
And being a shoulder to cry on
Thank you for giving so much of yourself
So much of your life to better mine
And thank you for playing such a large role
In shaping me
Into the father, husband and man I am today

...THEN TODAY HAPPENED

I thought

Maybe I was done

With writing for the year

With new sorrow for the year

It's the end after all

December

I thought

I could close this book

And start editing

Reading and rereading

I thought

The year would end on a positive

...then today happened

And I have to write

Because I have to process

While I sit alone in the car

I have to write that today you died

Today

Tonight

Tears in eyes

Your body just inside
Without life
With cuts
And blood
And so much left behind
So many whys

Six days before Christmas
December 19th
And two days ago
On the 17th
I said my last words to you
"I love you, brother
And I want good for you"
And you said you wanted to change
You told us all
But I guess everything
Was too much
The darkness
The sorrow from losing mom
The drugs
The paranoia
That you couldn't look past
Couldn't get over
And my heart breaks

For you and your son

That you felt this was the only way out

Things weren't always good between us

In fact, most of the time they weren't

But I love you

And I always wanted

And hoped for good for you

We all did

And I hope now

Because of a different choice

You made when you were a boy

That you have peace

For the first time

WHY, BROTHER

Why

Why did you do drugs

The first time

The second time

So many times

Why did you drink and drive

You got caught once

Twice

Three

Four times

Why'd you turn back to drugs

When mom lost her life

And harder ones this time

Why'd you have to make the choice

To not get help

And to take your life

Why'd you do that to him

Leaving behind a little boy

Your son

Why, brother

Why

UNSURE

Another loss

Another death

It feels like a button's been hit

A kind of reset

And I feel more sorrow

I feel more loss

Even more lost

And one of

The hardest things

Right now

For me

Is that

I'm just not sure

How to be

PROCESSING

The drugs took your mind
I think
Mania
Paranoia
Insomnia
They took your mind
And you took your life

UNKNOWING

It's so difficult

To know

How to properly process

And grieve

Four deaths in such a short time

Such a sudden change in our lives

So much looks different now

I want to know there's a proper way

But maybe there isn't

And I just have to try

And hope to get through this

Feeling lost

Flying blind

A VOICE IN THE DARK

Why am I so angry
It's his voice
In the dark
Using mine
To slowly pick at me
Judge me
And tear me down
From inside

HELD

Crawling

Near lifeless and broken

Torn clothes and skin

Bleeding, breathless, hopeless

Open wounds stinging

Slowing until

My aching arms give out

My face hits the ground

Tears soaking dirt

I choke

On kicked-up dust

And I don't know how

To continue

To pick myself up

I can't

I lie here

Hoping all is not lost

Crying softly

Alone

Until

You

Your gentle touch

Finds my shoulder

My waist

And so carefully, slowly

You turn me over

And pick me up

You see me

For me

And I'm loved

You see me

And envelope me

You sit where I had been

You sit on blood-stained,

Tear-soaked dirt

And you pull me close

So tight, secure

Like a child

I rest my head

Loved

I breathe deep

And I cry

EXPERIMENT

Hope for you
Was a failed experiment
I tried so many times

NEED OF YOU

I need you so much now

I want you to come for me

Though I know

You're already here

Waiting for me

To collapse into your arms

So you can hold me up

And wipe away my tears

But I don't know how

So please

Would you reach into the depths

Of sorrow and disgust

Grab my hands

And pull me up

Toward you

Wrap your arms around me

I need you so much now

NOT OKAY

I'm not fine
I cry
I hate (mostly myself)
And at times
I'm fake
Because I want to look okay

THINKING BACK

It can't have happened

He can't be slumped on the floor

Hope left me over the years

But there was a remnant

An ember

That always wanted more

It can't have happened

The remnant cut away with a knife

The ember doused in blood and tears

The end of his life

Everything ripped away

As the beating fades

Except for the one thing

That was always there

And will always remain

Love

From one to another

A deep, deep love

For my brother

A QUESTION

Who am I, really?
If most of the time
Most of my energy
Goes toward pretending

THANKFUL

I'm glad I have them

My friends

And my boys

I'm glad I have her

And I'm His

Because there's joy in those relationships

There's hope

Thankfully

Because lately

I often don't like myself

And feel miserable inside

FEAR

Sleep feels like a distant thing
Different than it used to be
When it came quickly in the night
Now it cowers when I reach
And I'm afraid
Of losing anyone else
So, I lie here
Eyes open
Staring into the dimly lit hallway

With our door open
I feel closer to them
To my boys
I stare and I pray that they're fine
And they are
I know this
But sleep won't come
And I'm afraid every night

TOO MANY

How many tears
In a year
Have I cried?
Too many to count
Too many to hide

PARANOIA

Your face

Speaking words

Theories

And paranoia

And you died

A week from that day

FALLING OVER THE EDGE

One tear

Then another

Filling lids

Of shame-filled eyes

Then more

Run and hide

Falling over the edge

Rolling down cheeks once dry

LOST AND ALONE

In a hole

Completely unwhole

Feeling lost

And alone

Something falls

And joins me

And more after

Piling on

And on and on

If only

I could pull myself free

And climb the pile

The edge

To open air

Where I could breathe

Instead, I struggle

Against the weight

Of things

I don't fully understand

MY HEART

My heart feels so heavy

It beats and feels

It aches

And it breaks

Shattered within me

And some days

It's all I can do

To keep my head

Above water

And just make it through

ALMOST

I almost hate you

Almost

But the blood

That soaked

A concrete floor

And spread about

A lifeless you

Is the same

As the blood

That flows through me

I almost hate you

But I don't

I loved you

I miss you

My heart breaks for you

I don't hate you

I just hate what you did

What you stole

WHAT DEATH SAYS

What does your death

Say about me

That in the strongest of ways

I hate when people leave

But your choice

Wasn't just a leaving

It was an abandoning

It was a final act

Way too early

With no encore

No hope for more

An end of your time

With any of us

An end of our time

With you

BETWEEN YOU AND ME

    There's no dealing with death
    Not when it's such
      a significant end
    An end to all things
    An end to a future
      between you and me

WILL AND WHY

Will good come from this

I hope so

I think so

I know so

Just not the how

Because right now

All I can think about

Is the why

END AND BEGINNING

'17 is coming to an end
and I look forward to '18
But just because one year ends
and a new year begins
doesn't mean grief and sorrow
are erased from our lives
And fresh grief has piled on the others
and I'll carry it all through the year
But
in spite of all the loss
All the tears
and questions
and anger
I'm ending the year well
With people who have been there for us
all year long
It's family
and friends like them
that have helped us through
It's shoulders we've cried on
Arms that have held us
It's listening ears

as we've tried to make sense
of our anger and heartache
These people have made moments great
in a year that was filled
with so many difficult ones
And I cry as I write
because I can't imagine
my life without them
Without their love and support
Thank you
Two words that feel far from enough
to say what our time together
and your words have meant to us
I love you
We love you
And we're better because of you